ARTIST TRANSCRIPTIONS PIANO

OSCAR PETERSON TRACKS

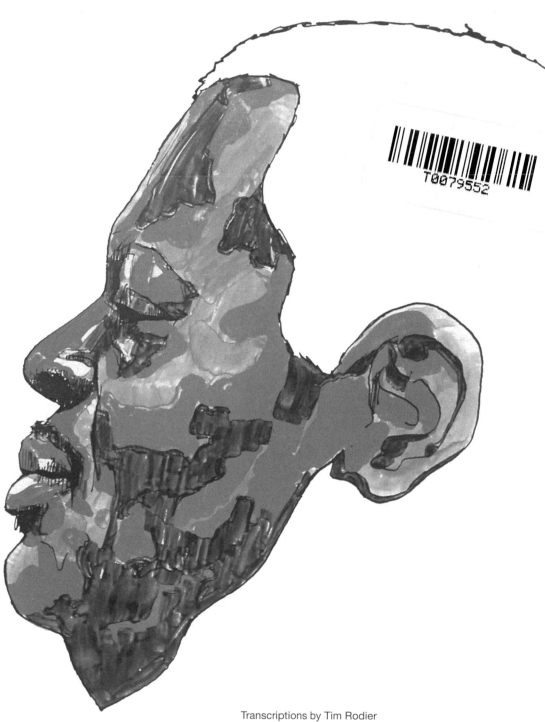

Transcriptions by Tim Rodier

ISBN 978-1-61780-428-1

HAL•LEONARD® CORPORATION

7777 W. BLUEMOUND RD. P.O. BOX 13819 MILWAUKEE, WI 53213

Visit Hal Leonard Online at
www.halleonard.com

Give Me The Simple Life

Words by Harry Ruby
Music by Rube Bloom

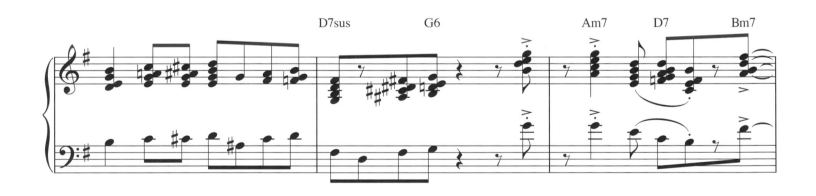

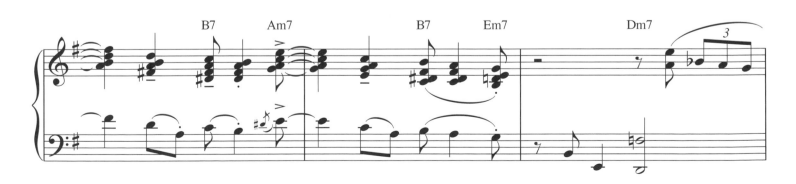

3rd Chorus

5th Chorus

Basin Street Blues

Words and Music by
Spencer Williams

20

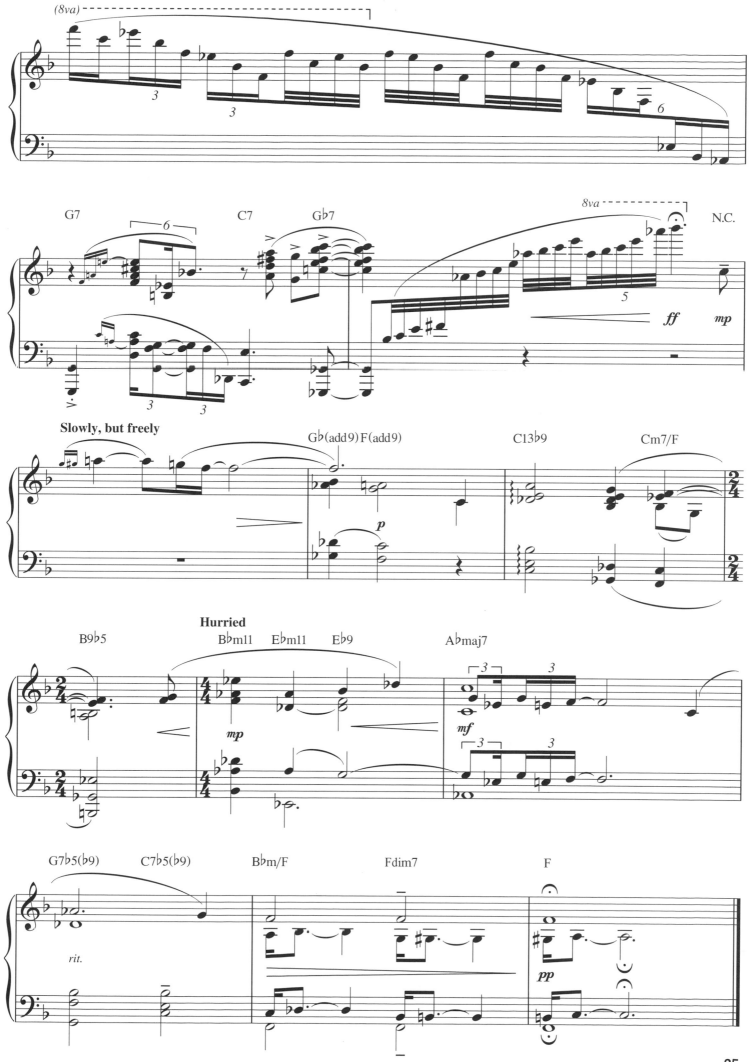

Honeysuckle Rose

Words by Andy Razaf
Music by Thomas "Fats" Waller

Dancing on the Ceiling

Words by Lorenz Hart
Music by Richard Rodgers

A Child Is Born

By Thad Jones

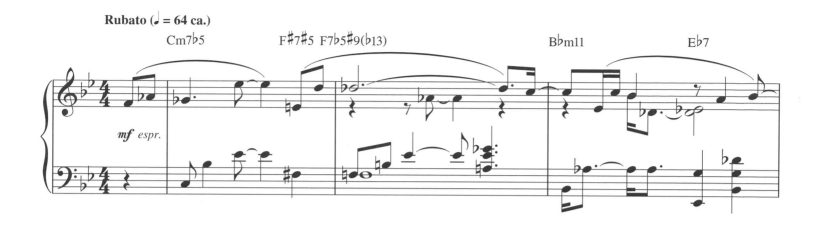

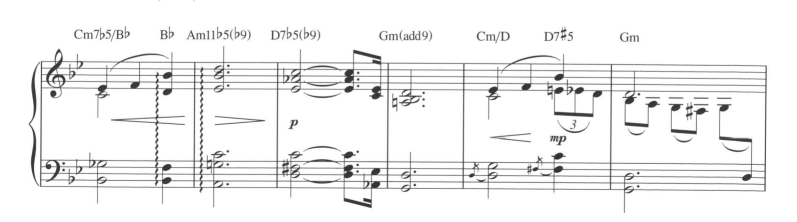

If I Should Lose You
from the Paramount Picture ROSE OF THE RANCHO
Words and Music by Leo Robin and Ralph Rainger

A Little Jazz Exercise

By Oscar Peterson

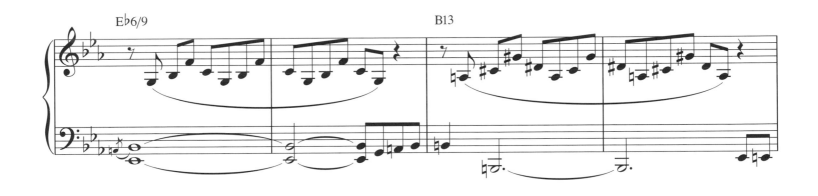

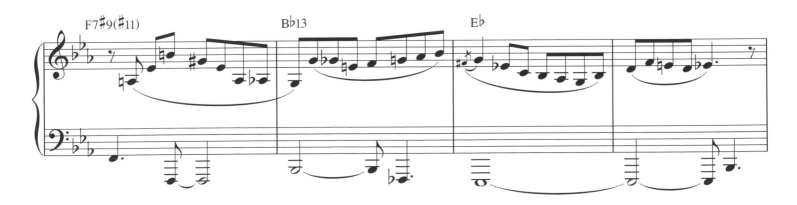

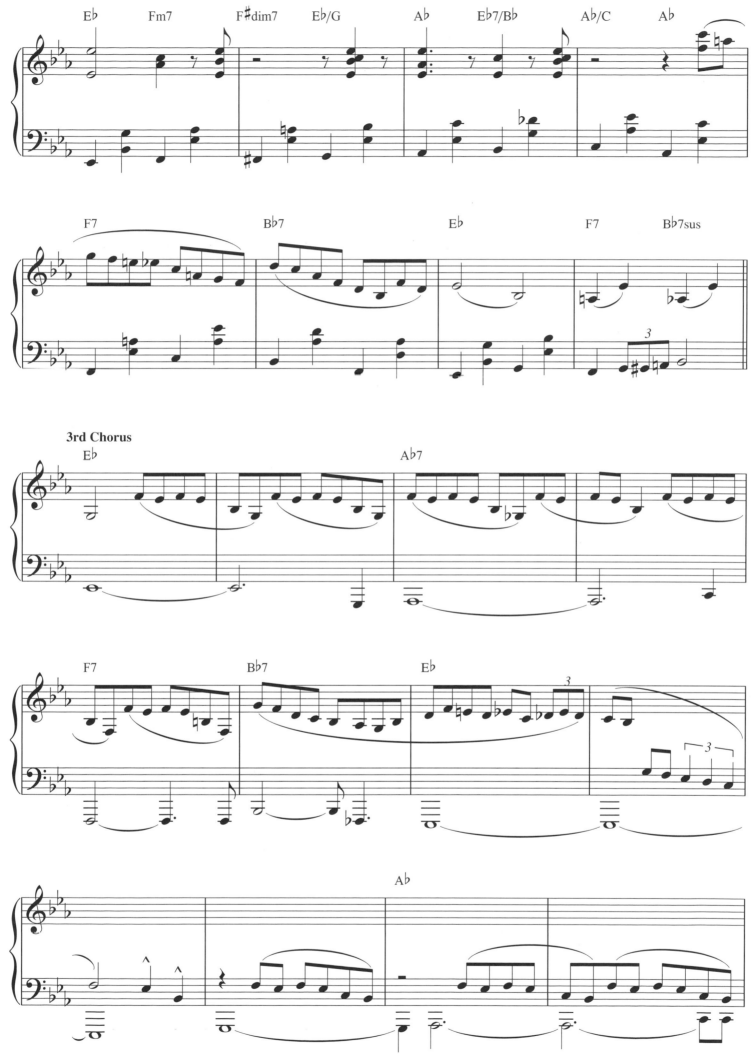

5th Chorus

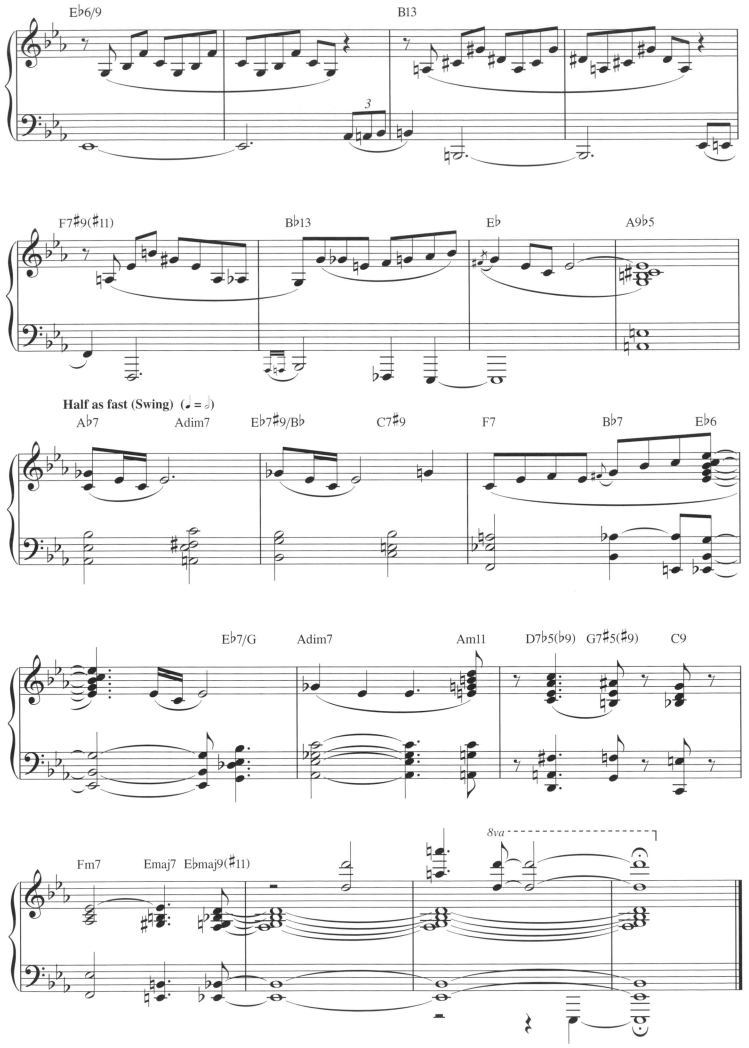

Django

By John Lewis

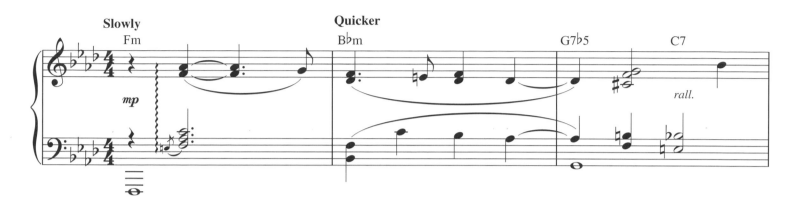

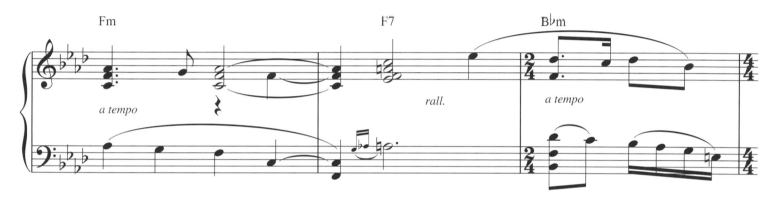

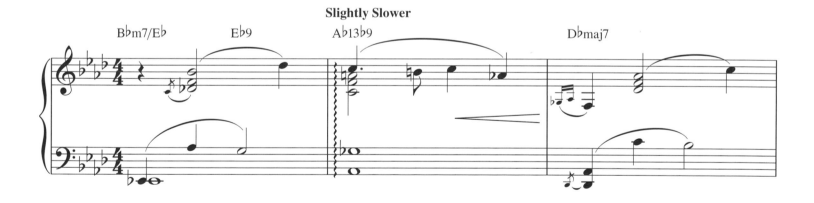

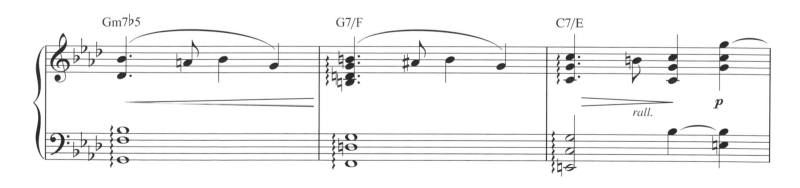

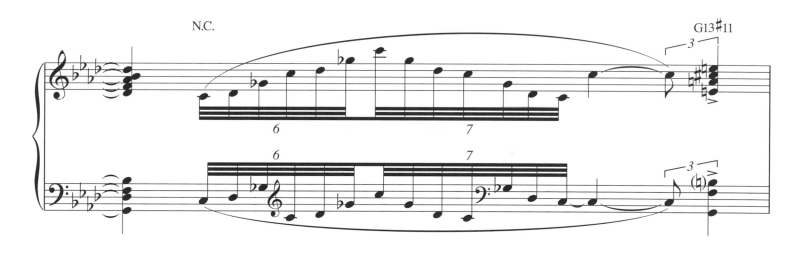

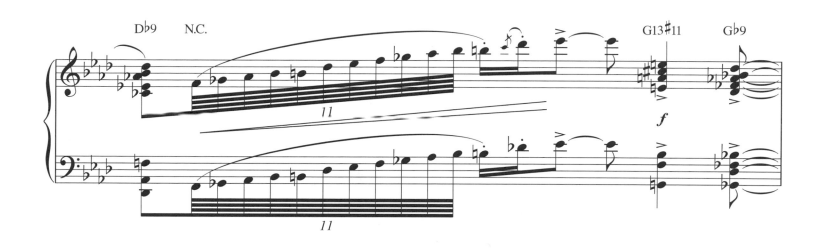

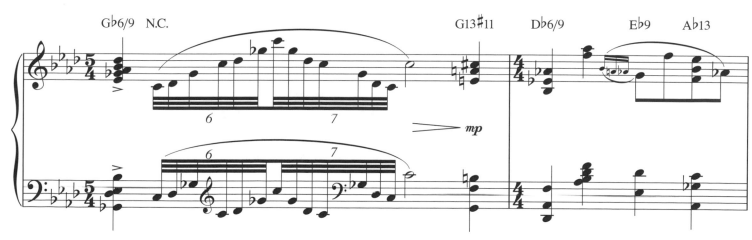

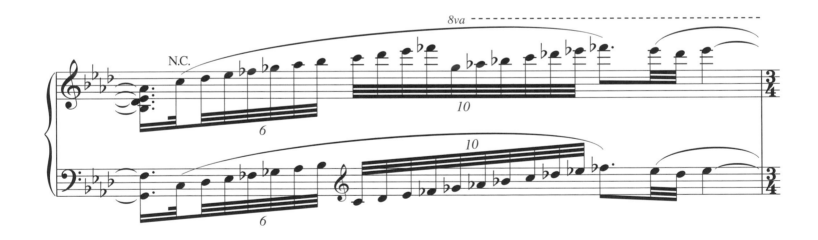

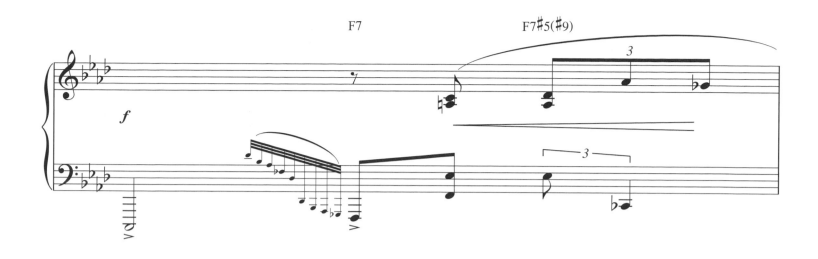

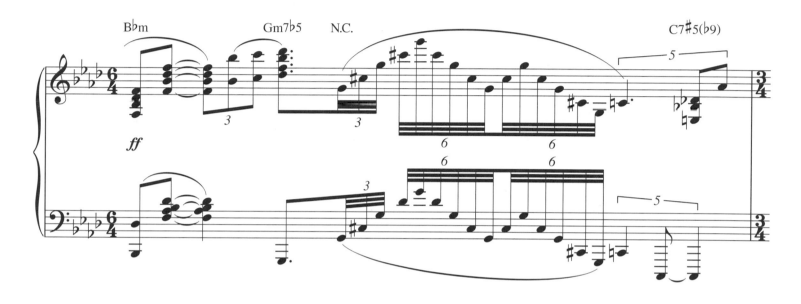

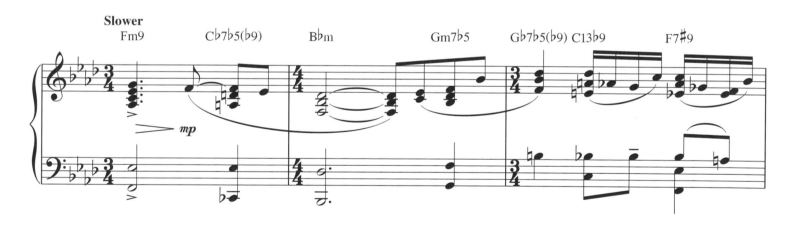

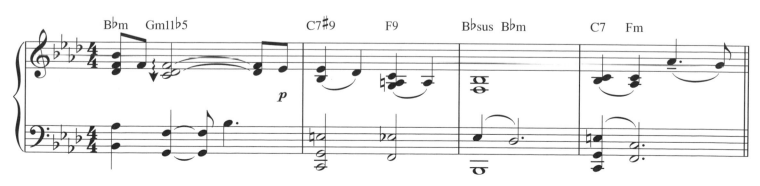

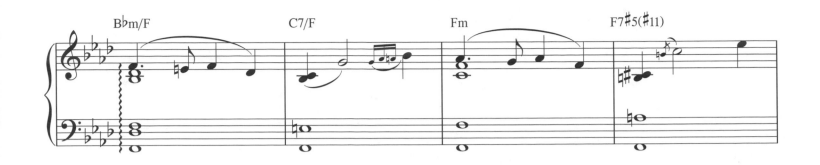

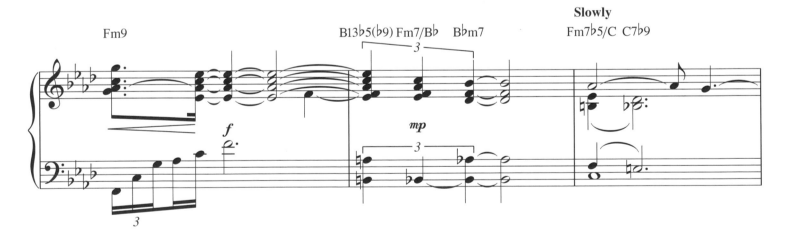

Ja-Da

Words and Music by Bob Carleton

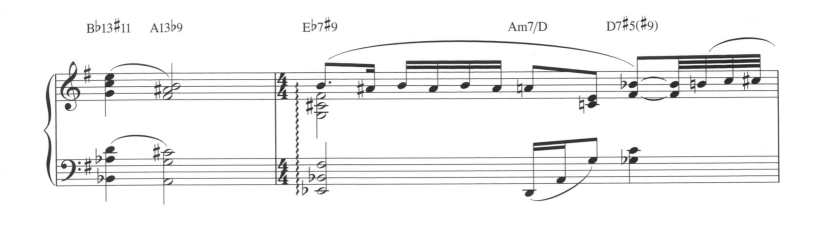

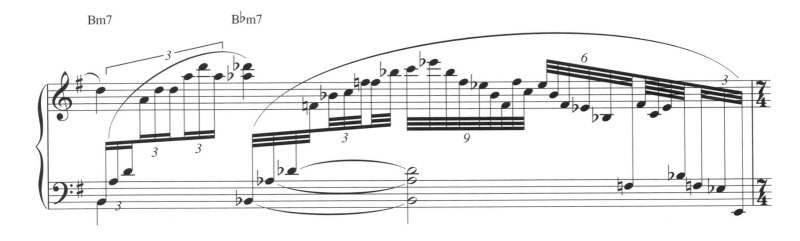

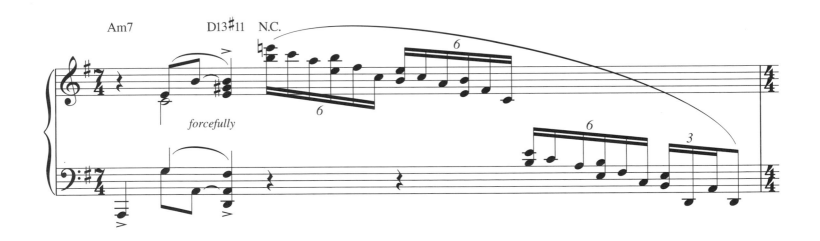

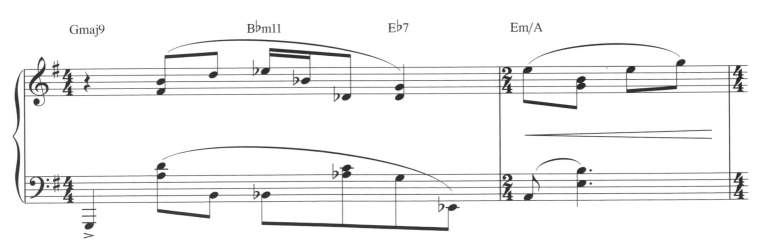

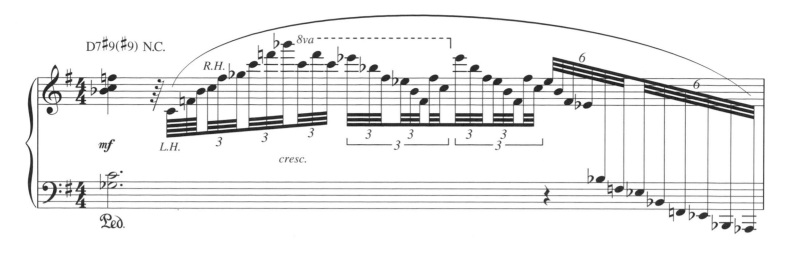

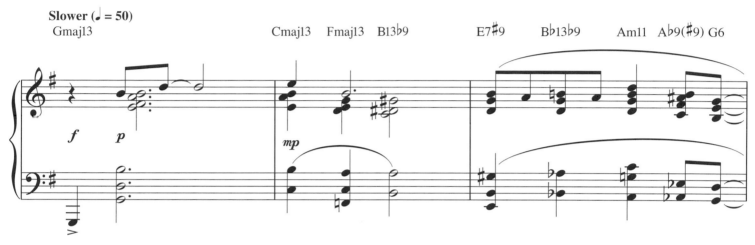

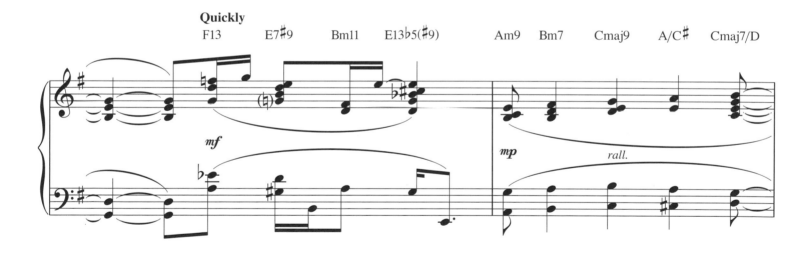

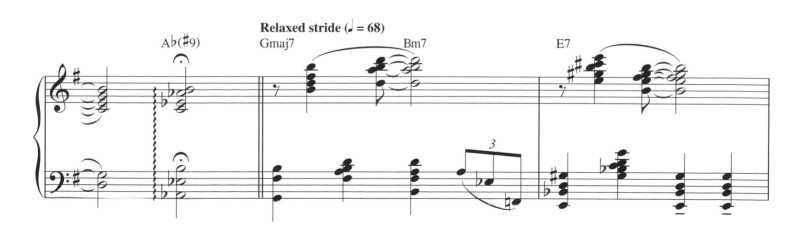

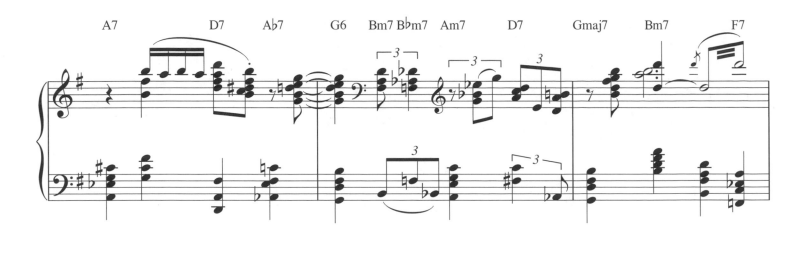

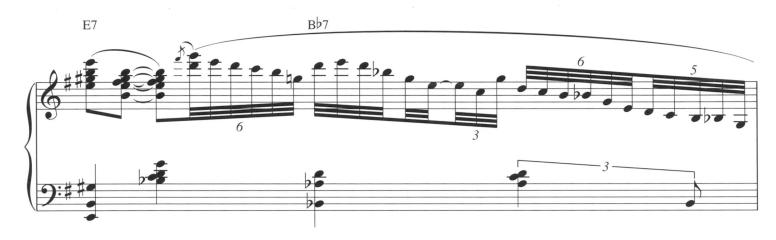

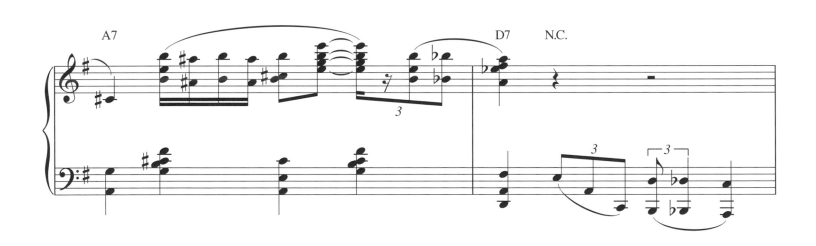

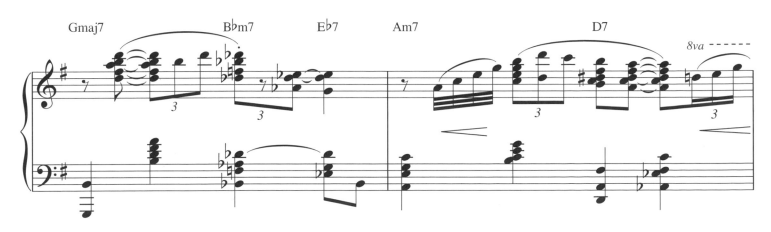

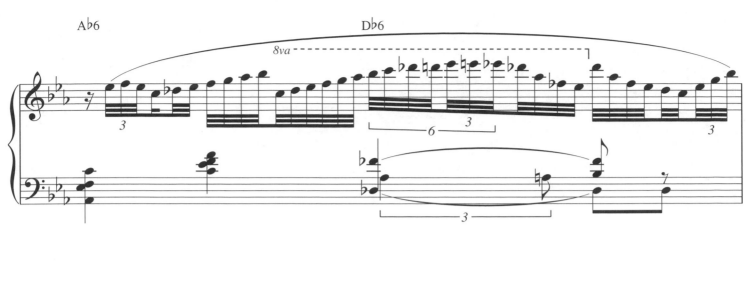

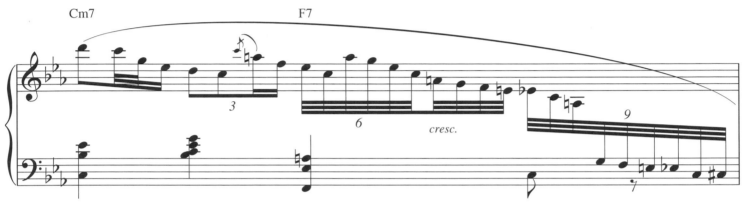

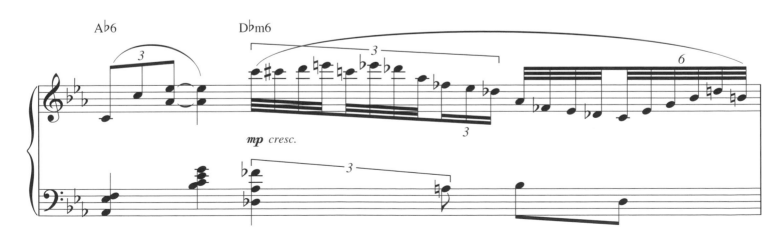

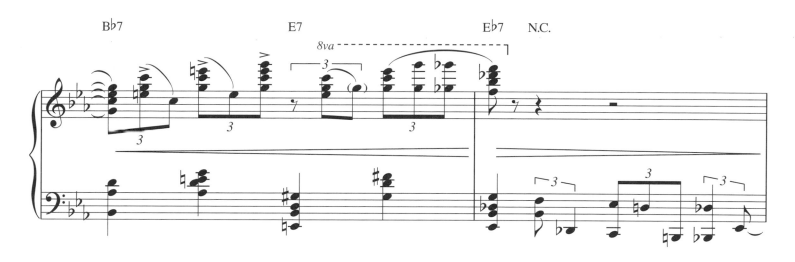

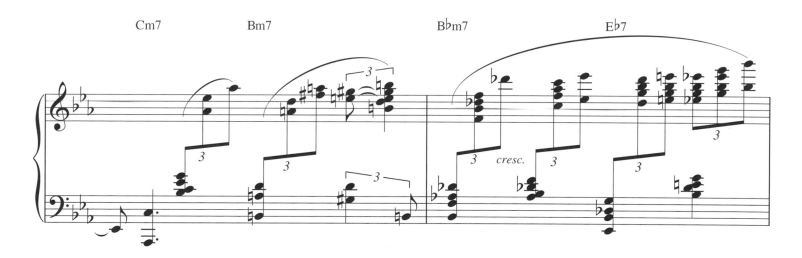

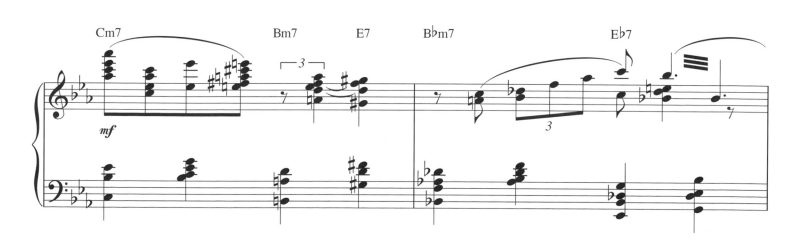

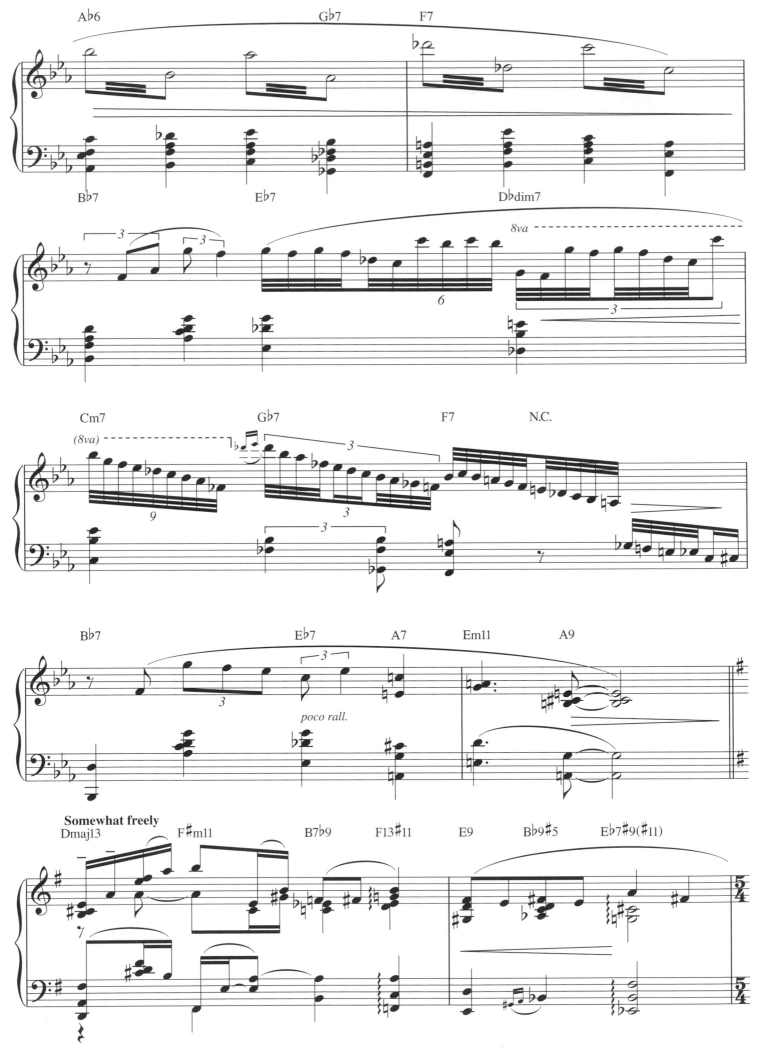

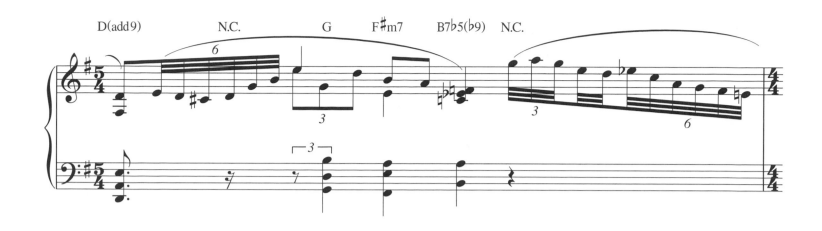

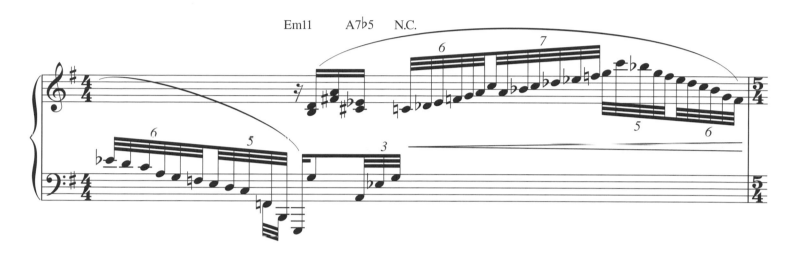

Just a Gigolo

Words and Music by Irving Caesar, Julius Brammer and Leonello Casucci

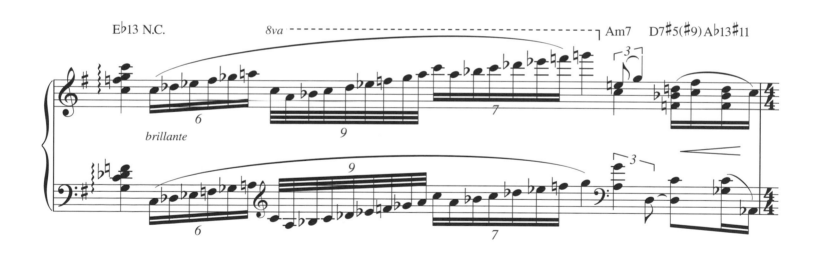

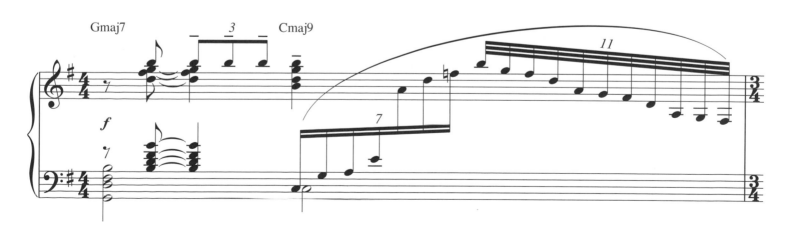

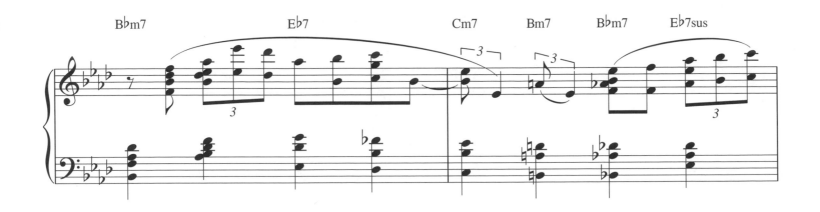

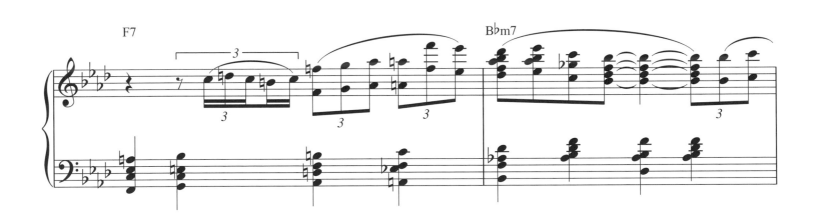

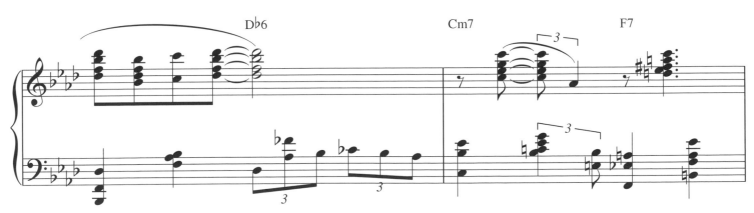

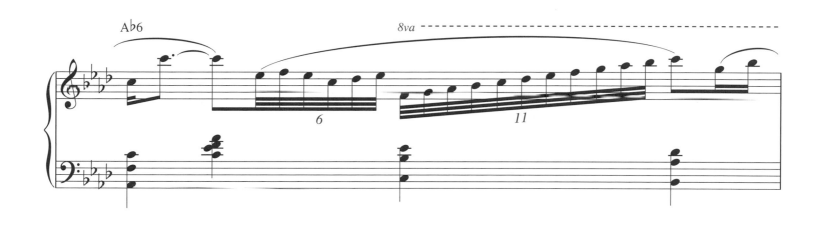

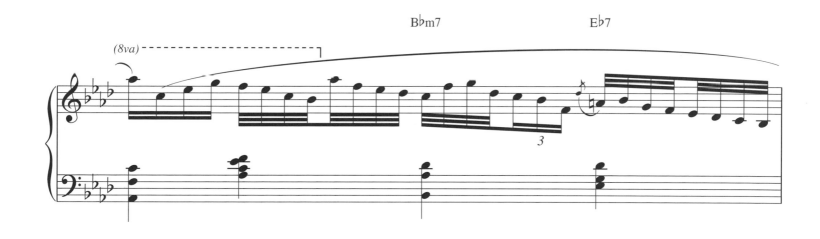

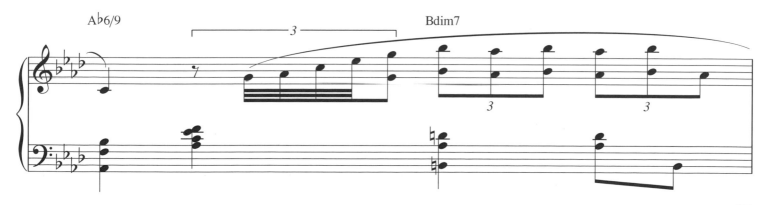

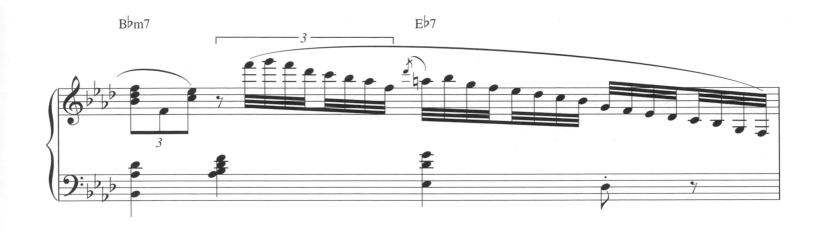

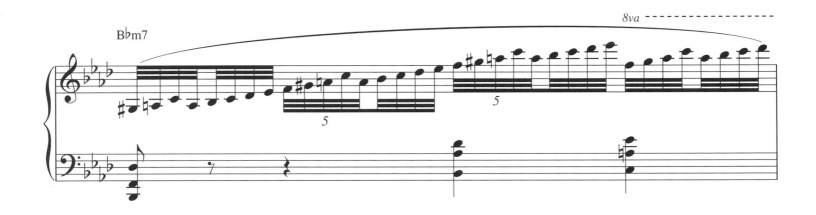

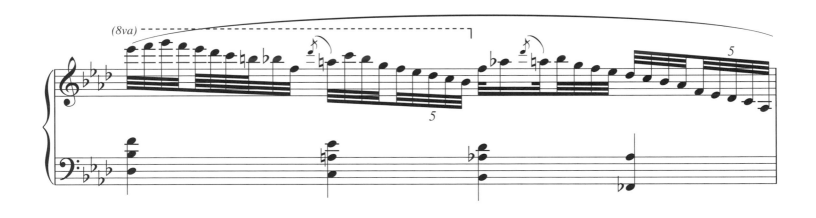

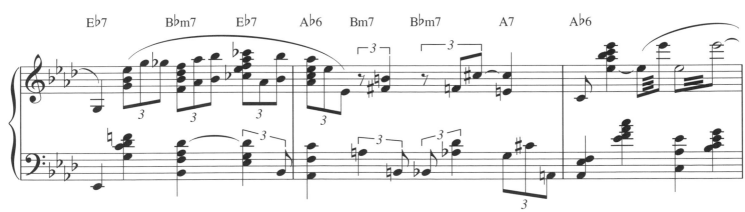

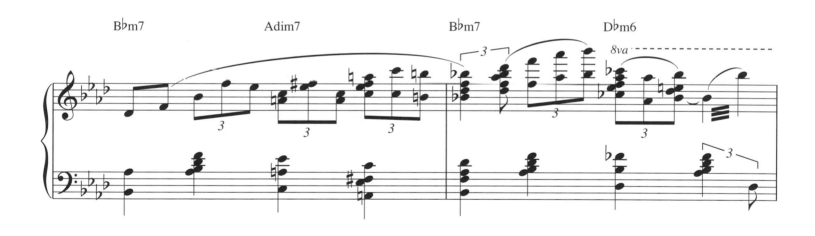

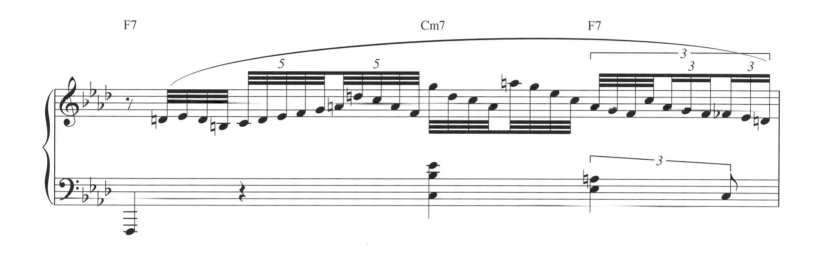

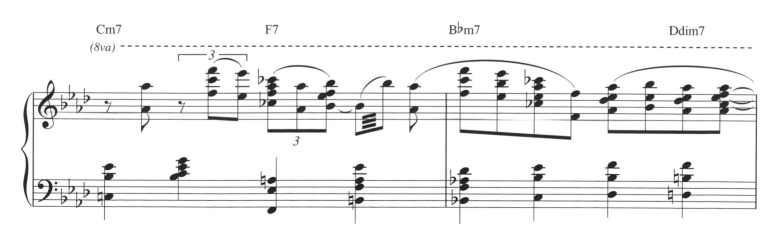

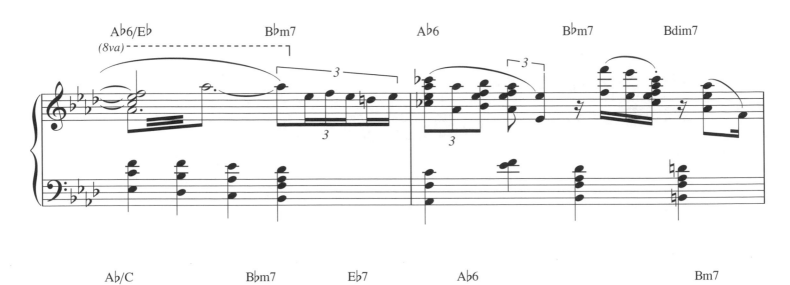

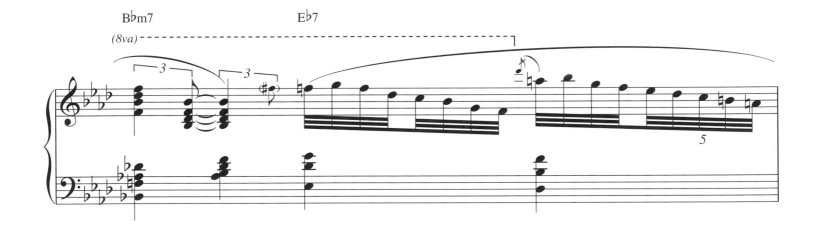

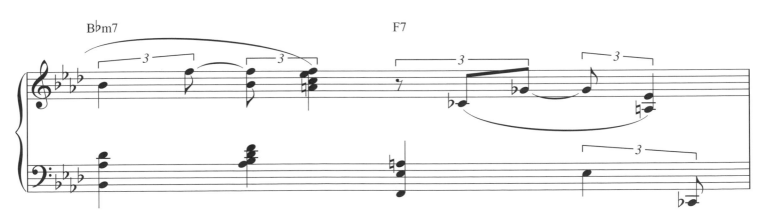

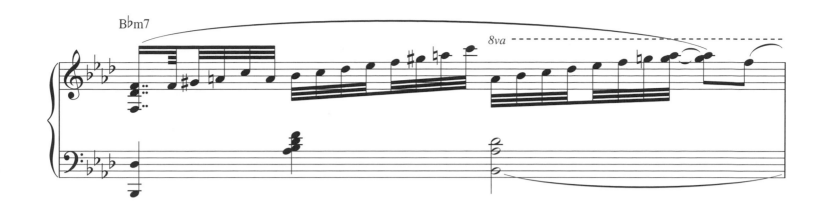

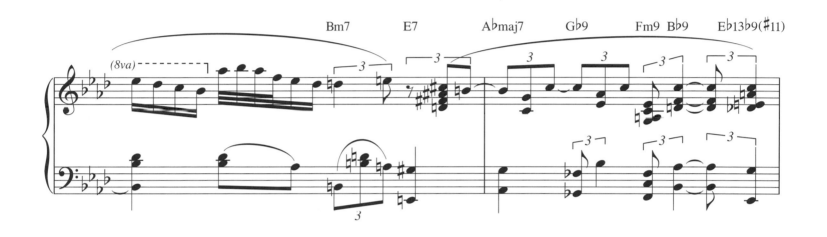

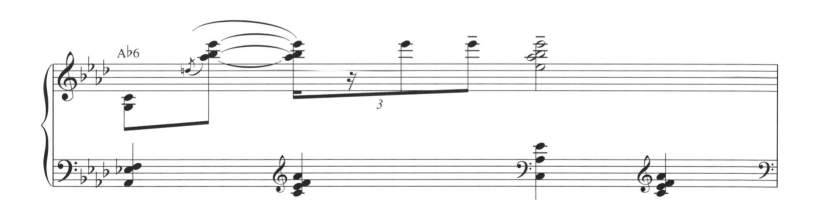

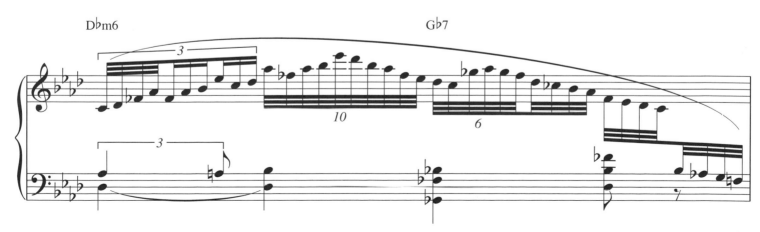

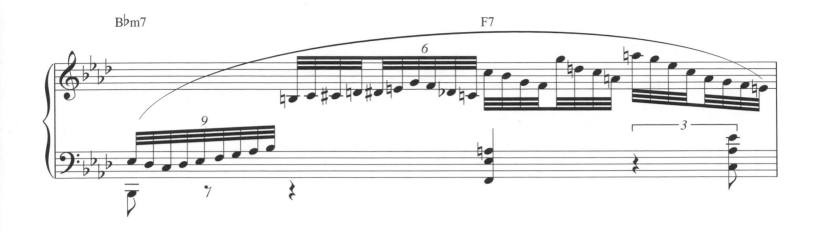

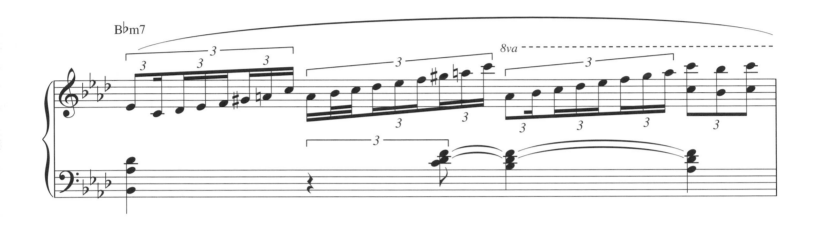

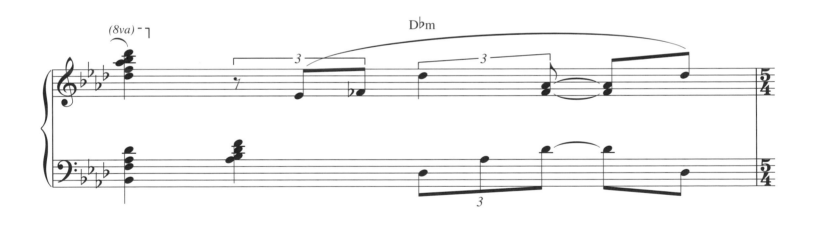

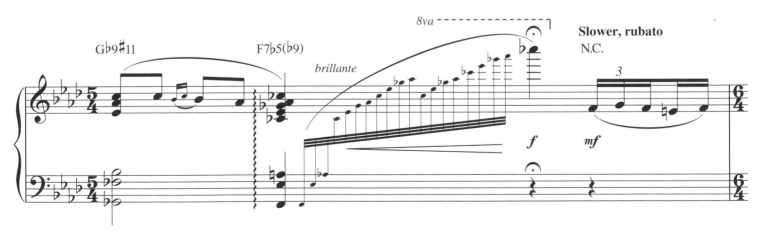

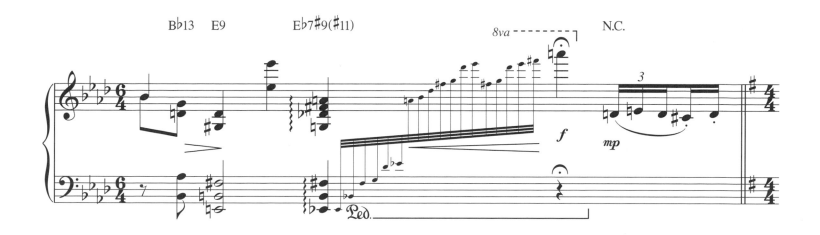

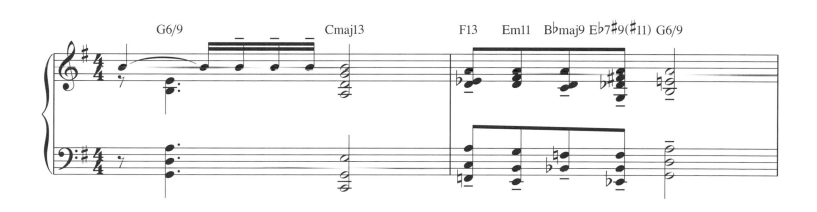

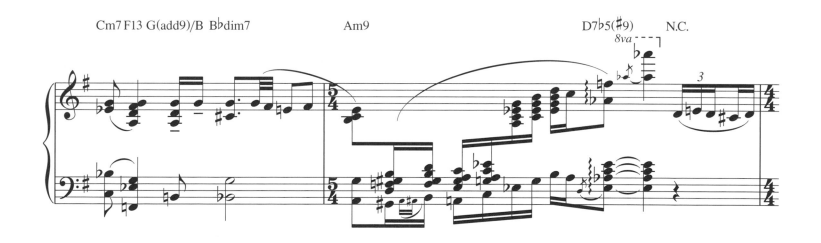

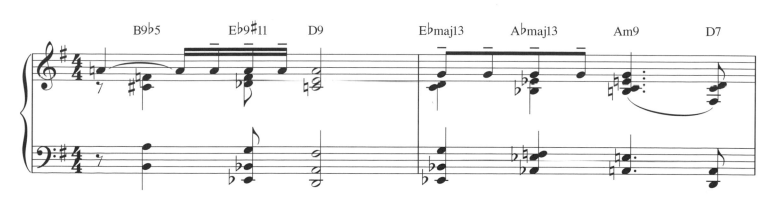

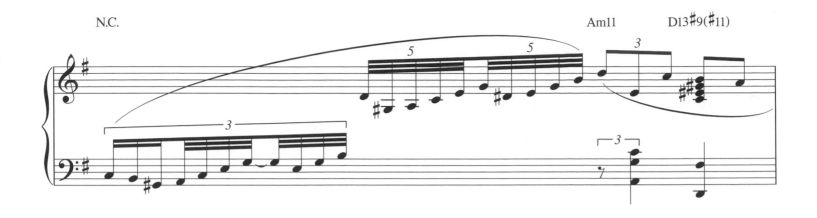

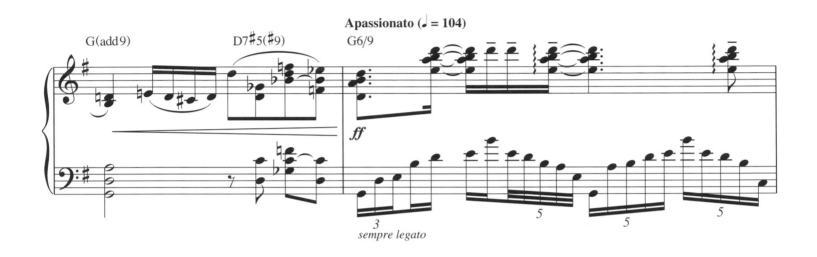

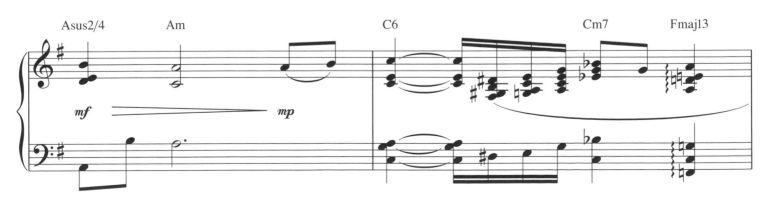

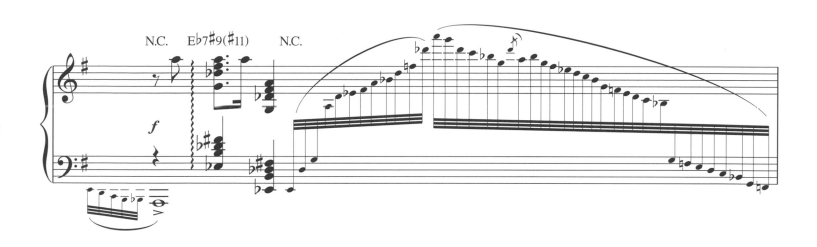

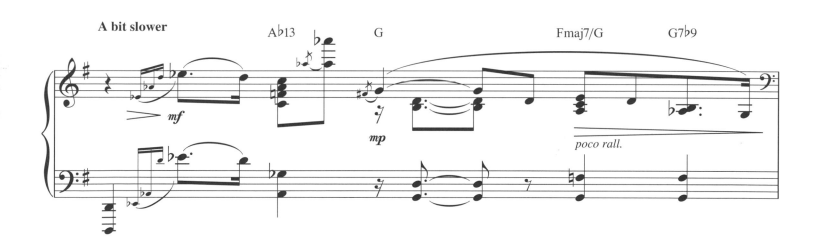

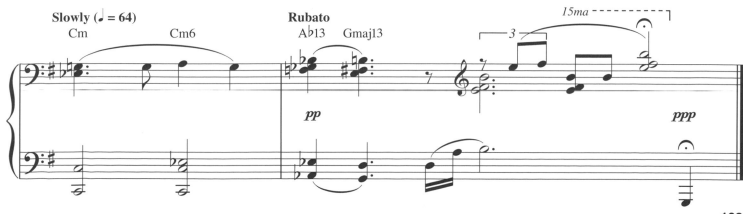